Ex-Wives and Ex-Lives:
Survival Guide
For The Next Wife

Paula J. Egner

Aptly Spoken Enterprises
"A word aptly spoken is like apples
of gold in settings of silver." (NIV) Proverbs 25:11

Published by Aptly Spoken Enterprises
19 Auburndale Cove, Jackson, Tennessee 38305

Printed in the United States of America

ISBN: 0-9752964-0-X
Library of Congress Control Number: 2004091314

Cover and interior design by Paula J. Egner

Visit our website at www.AptlySpoken.net

To my loving husband, Allen.
You've made me,
"Proud to be the Next-Wife!"

Author's Note

This publication reflects the author's opinion, and is written from the *next-wife's* point of view. It should be read like a letter from a friend, and not as from one who is rendering expert advice. If legal, marital, financial, or other counseling is required, the services of a qualified professional should be sought.

Many, but not all, typical *next-wife* scenarios have been exposed within these pages. They've been fictionalized from personal experiences, from a friend's lament, or from countless hours of listening to coworkers and acquaintances. **In each case, every identifiable detail has been modified to protect the participants' privacy (this includes names, number of children, age, and any other coincidental character or environmental situations).** However, the universal essence of the struggle within them, remains.

Contents

Chapter One:

Survive, Thrive... Or Demise?

Survival Ex-ism #1

EXpect

They say the battle's won
If you *expect* victory,
Keep your eye on the target;
You'll be shocked what you see.

You're not a bad person. Your friends have always said you have a kind heart. You've spent many holidays serving soup at the homeless shelter, and you're a charity solicitor's dream come true. You've consistently tried to follow the Golden Rule, and have made it a practice to offer forgiveness rather than to seek revenge. You've strived to be a genuine human being, worthy of the space you share on this earth with the rest of mankind.

But that image shattered when you married a man with a past. He'd been married before, and his ex-wife—his *ex-life*—trailed alongside him like a hideous appendage. Suddenly, thoughts of bitterness, of spite—or worse—sparked freely in your mind. Where had they come from? You'd never before wished anyone harm, and had no intention of starting now. But still, if his ex-wife could somehow *disappear* from his life—from your life— the relief would be intoxicating!

If you're pressed, you'd have to admit that you've envisioned her funeral more than once. In your mind's eye, you sat staunchly beside your husband—his rock during a difficult time—and consoled his children at their loss. With reverence and appreciation, you accepted the matriarchal torch her death passed to you. And your determination to create the perfect home for your new family, was only slightly tainted by the whisper of guilt you felt for being so happy.

But then you snapped back into reality and realized that her demise wouldn't really solve the problems you've had with your stepchildren. In fact, it might even make them worse by solidifying her martyrdom in their memory. No, you don't wish her harm at all. But you still hold onto the fantasy that one day, she'll be abducted by alien life forms and whisked away to another planet.

Your friends would be shocked if they knew how you've struggled with the anger, the resentment, perhaps even the hatred, toward the woman who shared your husband's life first. And the truth is, *you* can't believe it's you harboring those feelings! You knew about your husband's past before you married him, so why are you acting like all of this is such a surprise?

Because it is. No one prepared you for the facts of life in remarriage. They didn't explain with a knowing nod, that it isn't even close to the same game as a first marriage. If only a seasoned *next-wife* would've taken you aside before your remarriage nuptials. If she had explained the cold, hard truth to you, perhaps you would've listened and been better prepared for what lay in store. But alas, it's too late for that. The best you can hope for now is to learn the ropes as you're swinging from them. And pray that you won't miss the lifeline that's thrown to you.

In your attempt to teach yourself the survival skills you need, you've sought advice from a multitude of marriage books, to no avail. Most of them focus solely on first-timers. Even the Bible—the greatest help book of all time—doesn't directly address this confusing, emotional condition called being the *next-wife*.

However, as far back as the book of Genesis, the Bible does record the animosity that developed between Sarah and her servant, Hagar. Sarah's husband, Abraham, sired a son with the slave, and over a decade later, Sarah also bore him a male child. The women's jealousy and despise toward each other, spilled over and festered between the two boys. And as the children grew, their rivalry bred a murderous hostility that continues through their descendants to this day.

These two ancient women both had ties to, and a child from, the same man, although only one had the privilege of matrimony. That's not quite the same situation as a marriage and remarriage, but it's close.

Today's *next-wife* endures another woman having legitimate (or as the case may be, not-so-legitimate) access to her husband's time and attention. She graciously overlooks acquaintances making references to the first-wife in her presence. And she reminds herself that his children are still adjusting to the trauma of their parents' divorce, when they make no effort to hide their resentment that she's using up perfectly good oxygen with each breath she takes.

The wife in a first marriage seldom, if ever, has to deal with seeing her husband's ex-lover every other weekend. Rarely does she have to accept another woman calling him regularly at work to discuss a child that's theirs together. The first-wife gets him all to herself, free of encumbrances by another woman. She shares all of the important firsts with him—first house, first child, first promotion, etc.

The *next-wife* has to settle for something less. That's not to say that her husband doesn't love her— he does. Perhaps more than he's loved anyone in his life. He's matured to the point that he's able to appreciate their relationship, and considers himself fortunate at having found the love of a good woman (that would be you).

But the *next-wife* is probably the most misunderstood and least appreciated of all women. *Ex-Wives and Ex-Lives: Survival Guide for the Next-Wife,* is dedicated solely to this woman who came somewhere after the first wife (whether she's the second, third, or even the fourth wife). Within these chapters, you'll find insight into the very-real and much-denied *emotions* associated with not being first. You'll stomp all over the preconceived notions of how you "should" feel. And you'll reveal the festering blisters from walking in another woman's shoes.

If you're looking for a journal full of dry research, which underscores every psychoanalytical detail of being this unique woman, keep looking. You won't find that here. This isn't another predictable reference book that promises time will take care of all of your problems. True, time does help, but statistics state (okay, I'll need to cite just a few) that it takes anywhere from four to eight years for a remarriage and a new blended family to "gel." Can you make it that long without first driving yourself to the brink of madness—or to the depths of depression?

This survival guide is a practical, fresh look at the *real* problems and joys of being the *next-wife*, that could only be fleshed out by someone who has been one herself (more than once, actually). That doesn't make me an expert in marriage. If you want that, seek a marriage counselor.

At times, the blunt honesty may shock or appall you, but no longer will a *next-wife* suffer in silence for fear of society's retaliation. You now have a safe place to tell it like it really is.

Without a single thought of reprisal, you can finally admit that you not only don't love his children yet, but often struggle to even *like* them. And with your face totally expressionless and devoid of guilt or shame, you can admit how you wanted to cold-cock your new cousin-in-law, when the busybody inferred that your husband had married "down" from his first wife.

At last you'll speak out against socializing in the same circles that your husband and his ex-wife frequented. Even nature knows that sometimes, the old must be sacrificed on the altar of the new. A butterfly wouldn't get far if it insisted on dragging its cocoon along as it explored the skies. Neither will your husband be able to fly with you if he isn't willing to move on, unfettered from the past. He must leave some of his old life behind, in the interest of creating a new one with you.

You refuse to be a victim to fantasy and ill-preparedness any longer, and are determined to overcome the odds against you. In other words, your demise is not imminent. You are a survivor. And you'll thrive on this challenge called remarriage.

Ultimately, the art of being the *next-wife* requires a delicate balance between what has gone before, and what is yet to come. The Apostle Paul writes in Philippians 3:13, *"Brothers, I do not consider myself yet to have taken hold of it. But one thing I do: forgetting what is behind and straining toward what is ahead."* (NIV)

Amen! So be it. More than anything, the *next-wife* needs to aspire to this ideal of pressing onward.

Chapter Two:

Next Up

Survival Ex-ism #2

EXplore

Stretching out beyond
You *explore* a world unknown,
Though wrought with pits and snares;
It's the place you now call home.

You're not his first love. You weren't his first choice, and you never will be. You're the enigma called the *next-wife*. You're legally entitled to wear his name, yet must forever bear the stigma of not being the *first* woman to do so.

And the truth is, he wasn't your first choice, either. Although men have typically been accredited with being able to compartmentalize their lives, you're the one who has neatly tucked your past away, like a memento in a drawer. You may have occasionally stumbled upon it, and perhaps even reminisced briefly. Still, you've never allowed it to interfere with your current happiness.

Your new husband's ex-life was much more complicated than that. And his ex-wife was none too happy about your union, either. But, you were certain that you'd at last found your soul mate when you found your new love. The past was but a distant memory for both of you. Your bright future together was all that mattered, right?

Yeah, right! And Elvis was spotted singing hymns on Beale Street last Sunday morning.

19

Your past is the brick and mortar that built who you are today. To minimize the impact it's had on your present life, is akin to foolishly spitting into the wind just because you can't see it. Ironically, that same past has also laid the foundation for your future happiness.

Your husband came with much more than just the years ticked off by his age. He also brought an ex-wife along, and minor or adult children. In other words, he came with an *ex-life*. And any woman who doesn't believe that all of them become part of the remarriage union, has either never been remarried, or has never been divorced.

If your new husband's former marriage didn't produce children, he should have no reason to continue a relationship with his ex-wife. In this case, his former marriage can truly be chalked up to a learning experience, and he can move on as a free man. When you become his next-wife, your experience should be like vanilla ice cream, instead of the fifty-seven flavored sludge this book describes.

Remarriage with children requires the continued presence of the ex-wife. It's not a pretty sight. But then, divorce is an ugly thing, and no matter how much we don't want to admit it, most remarriages are founded on divorce. Therefore, the situations addressed herein are all based on the first wife being alive and kicking. Sometimes literally.

Currently, half of all marriages are not *original*—that is, it's not the first coupling for the spouses. It's a remarriage for one or both of them. And yet, there are few resources that deal with the unique challenges that remarriage inevitably poses, especially for the woman-half of the new union.

The *next-wife* could be compared to being the pageant runner-up, who was crowned only after the original winner relinquished her title. This second-placer is now legitimately the queen, but was denied the satisfaction of having prevailed over all contestants originally. Her victory is hollow. Likewise, though the *next-wife* reigns in his heart now, she will be forever denied her rightful place as his first choice.

Intellectually, you realize that life isn't a contest, and as such, cannot be orchestrated as one. Most likely, there was never any competition between you and his former wife at all. And you've consoled yourself that she isn't a threat to you now, either. At least, that's what others have told you, (well-meaning friends who have never been married, or who are still in their first marriage, anyway). And perhaps what they've said is true. Or maybe not.

You've told yourself that she couldn't be all bad since both of you had the same taste in men. Yet that reasoning is chased away by one ugly question that plagues you—*What did he ever see in her, anyway?*

So you've continued your lonely struggle with just where you fit into the grand scheme of your new husband's complex life, and into your life together.

And you may have felt isolated in your efforts to overcome some of the most common situations, that you'll soon realize, most *next-wives* have experienced.

You may be surprised to discover that becoming a *next-wife* has forged you into being one of the most creative, resilient, thick-skinned women on this planet. In spite of all the obstacles, you've remained an unsinkable optimist. And no naysayer can convince you otherwise.

So let's get down to the business of just what it means for the woman who marries a man who has an ex-wife (or two) and ex-lives to match. Just who is this mysterious woman called the *next-wife*?

Buckle up—you're about to run headlong into reality!

Chapter Three:

Signs of the Times

Survival Ex-ism #3

EXchange

Perhaps you should've seen
Your situation more clearly,
But you *exchange* the illusion;
For the man you love dearly.

There were signs. You saw them sprouting up like weeds along the highway of your courtship. Occasionally, you even slowed down long enough to inspect them closer. But their fragrances were cleverly disguised as sweet perfume, and lulled you into a false sense of security. Oblivious to the potholes that lay ahead, you quickly resumed your devil-may-care ride toward remarriage.

You were in love, and perhaps a bit cocky. Nothing was going to get in the way of your newfound happiness. Most of all his ex-wife.

In hindsight, perhaps you should've realized that she wasn't going to just disappear the closer you and your new love came to remarriage. Quite the opposite, in fact. Instead, she became like an apparition, popping out from the shadows of your new life, her palpable presence dampening holidays and birthday celebrations, though she wasn't physically there.

Of course, not all ex-wives fit this description. Many pride themselves on not interfering with their ex-husbands' new lives. Some ex-wives seem to have

25

little problem embracing the thought that their ex-husbands have remarried. This type of woman has come to terms with her own less-than-perfect past, and has moved on with her life. She is only grateful that his new wife (that would be you) is good to her children (let's hope that you are).

Unfortunately, *your* ex-wife is not one of these! You may have noticed the use of the possessive pronoun here. That's because referring to your husband's former spouse as *your* ex-wife, instead of *his,* seems to be most appropriate. Mysteriously, new husbands tend to tone out most everything she says or does (perhaps from years of practice?), leaving you to do most of the dirty dealing with the former missus. In any case, she has become the proverbial thorn in your flesh, and one that continues to prick your good-natured disposition, no matter how hard you try to ignore her.

As you journey through the pages of this book, allow yourself to feel the presence of your *next-wife* "sisters." Although each situation is as individual as the woman living in it, the knowledge that you are not alone, may be just the catharsis that will extract the ex-wife from her festering place of irritation in your life.

But what were the signs that this woman would become such an integral part of your future? After all, you married her ex-husband, not *her.* How could you have known that her very existence would taunt you for years to come? Below are some of the signs that you might recall from when you were cruising down that carefree road of courtship.

1. *The Ex-wife Called Your Acquaintances.* She discovered that her ex-husband was seeing you seriously, and set out to destroy the budding romance. Her hit-list included your ex-husband, your business associates, fellow church members, etc. Her intent might've been to dig up dirt on you, or just the age-old vindictiveness of gossip. Perhaps she hoped that the tentacles of this bizarre behavior would choke the life out of her ex-husband's interest in you. Surely his enlightenment about your past would seal the demise of your relationship forever. If she included the children—either minor or grown—in her antics against you, her behavior gave way to something much more sinister. Imagine the serpent in the Garden of Eden, twisting what God had told Adam and Eve into his own camouflaged words of death and destruction. You get the picture.

2. *The Ex-wife Confronted You in Public.* Perhaps she interrupted you and your new love while you were having a romantic dinner in a quaint restaurant. Her

theatrics succeeded in gaining her the attention of onlookers, as well as leaving a sour taste on your palate.

3.   *The Children Suddenly Turned Against You.* Strange, but you could've sworn that they liked you the first six months you dated their dad. So what happened? *Sniff* Smells like their mother realized that their father was serious about you. She moved the queen piece in her chess game of manipulation, and guess who became perfect pawns?

4.   *She Tried to Rekindle the Relationship With Her Ex-Husband.* There isn't a lot that the *next-wife* can do about this maneuver. It's totally up to her new love to squelch any sparks his ex may have tried to ignite. Of course, if he didn't snuff them out, you probably never became his *next-wife*, anyway.

5.   *She Called You and Wanted to be Friends.* She may or may not have ulterior motives, but before you jump onto the friendship bandwagon too fast, first ask yourself one question: Do you really want to be close friends with a woman who has seen your husband *naked*? *Hmm.*

Called Acquaintances

Many times you've rehearsed how you were going to tell that woman off! And you just might have done it, too, except you knew it would've given her more satisfaction if she'd known that she'd upset you.

But how did you find out what she'd been up to? It's called playing both sides of the fence. Those people she'd contacted had also been anxious to straddle that gossip picket! They'd been allowed a sneak-peek into your private life, and would've been all too happy to continue their social voyeurism, by hearing your side of the story. Of course, they'd mentioned what his former spouse had done, under the guise of something you needed to know for your own good. But what they really wanted, was to see what juicy tidbits you might expose about the ex-wife in return. This would make a heck of a reality television show!

This whole scenario can be embarrassing and damaging, especially if you truly do have dirty underwear hanging out in the breeze now. But it's not the end of the world. Usually the fear of exposure is much worse than the exposure itself. And once it's out in the open...well, you can't get much more private than dirty underwear, so the power of her punch fizzles from here.

And you haven't endured this humiliation for nothing. Your new love most likely saw a major character flaw in his ex that may have gone unnoticed previously. After all, no one likes a bully. And if, in fact, you had nothing to do with the disintegration of your new love's former marriage (which is the assumption throughout this book) then that's exactly what she was—a bully.

Her attempt to scare you off not only didn't work, it actually backfired. Although your new love defended your right to retaliate, he fell even more deeply in love with you when you wouldn't lower yourself to her level. He saw the depth of your character in a tough situation, and was drawn even closer to you than before.

You wish you could flaunt *that* fact in her face. But you won't.

Public Confrontation

This is the stuff of movies and novels. Your new love's ex caused a scene publicly, somehow believing that all of the humiliation would be cast upon the objects of her scorn (that would be her ex-husband and you), yet remarkably, bounce off her completely. Of course, nothing was further from the truth. Her targets may have suffered, but she didn't emerge from the battle unscathed, especially in the eyes of those who witnessed her outburst.

So what can you do about it? Not much, except refuse to participate in the drama. Period.

Sit there silently, even smile if you can bear to. Or get up and leave. Whatever is necessary to diffuse her attack. Just *don't* compound her pettiness by joining in the name-calling or accusation-throwing behavior. The mark of maturity is self-discipline, and it will require all you possess not to reciprocate with remarks of your own.

The ex-wife will have succeeded only in fueling the gossip funnel about her own childishness and poor judgment. And your new husband will once again, see how his future *next-wife* displayed tolerance and self-control in a volatile situation. Ironically, his former spouse's theatrics will have nudged her ex-man even closer to you.

Remember, womanly maturity seduces; childish tantrums repulse.

His Children Turned Against You

Heather had been dating Drew for several months, and in the process met his seven-year-old son, Thad. The boy took to her immediately. She played basketball with him on the hoop in his dad's driveway, and he soaked up the attention that she easily bestowed upon a child so young.

Their relationship was going quite nicely, until one fateful day Thad naively told his mother about his dad's new girlfriend. He explained how pretty Heather was, and how she played games with him on the weekends he visited his father.

Heather eventually married Drew, and Thad became her stepson. But their relationship was strained forever after his earlier confession to his mom. Thad's mother had used her son as a convenient dumping ground for her bitterness and anger about Drew and his new love. And when she'd heard the news of the remarriage, she'd also heaped guilt upon the boy's young shoulders. He accepted the burden that friendship with Heather, meant disloyalty to his mom, and refused to have a relationship with his dad's *next-wife,* thereafter.

If you've experienced a similar situation, there is hope for a happier ending than the one I just described. After seven years of remarriage and of being at constant war with the ex-wife, Heather and Drew divorced. Sadly, their coupling wasn't the only casualty. Thad had suffered debilitating depressions throughout his preadolescent years, and his schoolwork and social interactions were impaired as a result.

If you're one of the fortunate few that have an ex-wife who listens to reason, and places the well-being of her children above her bent on revenge, then you may be able to discuss the situation with her and work out a solution. Regretfully, too often this isn't an option. In that case, there are professionals who specialize in helping children work through the emotional trauma of their parents' divorce.

Regardless of how you choose to handle this

dilemma, remember one note of caution—*never* bad-mouth the child's mother to him, or even within earshot of him. (You'd be surprised just how broad a hearing range he has when he's at your house!) That includes your facial expressions and body language at the mention of her name.

Dealing with the complexities of stepchildren will be addressed in more depth in a later chapter.

Attempts to Rekindle Romance

Divorced couples often have a hard time completely letting go of their former spouses. Phone calls and occasional visits may continue long after the divorce is final. However, this behavior usually plays itself out naturally, and is history by the time either ex begins dating someone seriously. If you discover that your new love hasn't discontinued his practice of late-night phone conversations, or of spending special occasions with his ex-wife—*run!* Clearly, he's not ready for you!

As a disclaimer, some divorced couples *are* able to maintain a platonic friendship, though they're clearly in the minority. Therefore, they are not considered in this scenario.

Having said that, how close is *too* close for your new love to be to his ex-wife? Some women have a much higher tolerance level for close encounters of the "ex" kind, than others do. A lot also depends on the nature of the relationship you have with your new man. But rest assured, if your gut clenches when he tells you that she's called him yet again at work to discuss some trivial matter, trust your *instincts*—not her.

But she divorced him, you say! If she'd have wanted him, she would've kept him! Tsk, tsk. You really need to study basic ex-wife anatomy. The issue isn't whether or not she wanted him, it's that now you could replace her forever in his life.

Don't be naïve. Even if she doesn't want to remarry him, that doesn't mean she's going to sit idly by and watch him be happy with another woman.

And what about her children? As their mother, surely she has an obligation to protect them and their inheritance, from the likes of a gold-digger like you! If that protection requires her continued presence in her ex-husband's life, so be it.

Ultimately, there's not a lot you can do about this situation except see it for what it is. You can stand up for yourself and refuse to play second-fiddle to his ex-wife, but it's still up to your new love to handle her overtures. And when he takes the necessary stance against her romantic endeavors and draws even closer to you, the situation will have, yet again, only proven to strengthen your love for one another.

Friend or Foe?

There's a big difference between being cordial and being friends. No one can tell you with whom you should or should not be friends, but being cordial when at all possible, ranks right up there with the Golden Rule. It fits somewhere in the etiquette pages of how to be a decent human being.

However, that doesn't mean you must become close friends with his ex-wife. Will you be comfortable confiding intimate secrets to someone who used to sleep in your husband's bed, and who shares children with him? Having an amicable relationship with his ex, without crossing the line over into friendship, may be sufficient. There's no need to muddle over into the realm of intimacy with her.

One couple actually spent the night in the same vacation one-room cabin, with the man's ex-wife and her new husband. They were practically toe-to-toe in their separate beds! The two children shared by the "original" couple were also present. This is a classic example of trying just a little too hard! The children were confused, and their loyalties were divided four ways.

As long as no one is worried that there'll be a blowup whenever the ex and *next-wife* are thrown together (by athletic events or special occasions), you've probably reached that healthy plateau of cordiality. Stay in separate rooms, and leave the slumber parties and *best* friends to the children.

35

So, you've seen the signs and have believed! Yet you weighed the costs, and remarriage to your new love still beckoned. You officially became his *next-wife*, and innocently embarked upon uncharted territory. You moved out of your old neighborhood and into his, and into a higher level of personal growth. You birthed a whole new way of life. But the gestation period stretched your limits until you feared you'd pop!

Bear down, because your greatest labor of love is yet to come.

Chapter Four:

Out of Step

Survival Ex-ism #4

EXpand

You step out in the usual way—
Dance the familiar song,
Turn, twist and *expand*;
'Cause the old steps are all wrong.

Congratulations! You're now a stepmom, whether to minor or adult children. However, they didn't come packaged as tiny pink or blue bundles of joy, but rather as psychedelic conundrums. Your head aches as you try to figure out these riddles called stepchildren.

The only stepmother role models you've known, were a wicked character in a fairy tale, or the sugary-sweet sitcom ideal. Still, you believe reality lies somewhere in between those stereotypes. You're sure it'll all come down to common sense. After all, your new husband's children are part of him, and therefore you'll love them as if you'd actually given them birth. *Of course* you'll treat them like you would treat your own children, which will include not only loving them, but instructing, nurturing, and disciplining them when necessary.

That's your first mistake! You don't have the luxury of thinking of them like they're your own. You must view them not only as your husband's children, but also as his ex-wife's offspring. And that means that you'll be expected to treat them *better* than you'd treat your own flesh and blood! They'll be allowed to get away with more shenanigans than you could dream of, solely because the ex-wife threatened to take your husband back to court to reduce his visitation schedule, if he allowed you to discipline them again.

But you argue that your natural children are the sparkle in your eye. You love them more than life itself! Although you swear you would never show favoritism to them over your stepchildren, there's also no way you could treat another woman's children better than you treat your own.

No one ever warned you about the bitter truth of stepmothering, did they? You had no idea that from the moment you said "I do," you'd be expected to view his little devils as incarnate angels.

And you'd naively assumed that since you were a good mother, you would naturally become a wonderful stepmother. That was another hard-earned lesson you were taught early in your remarriage journey. The two positions are similar in name only. Their real functions are worlds apart.

As a mother, you probably desire to be friends with your children. Yet you take the responsibility of being their parent seriously, and acknowledge that being their mother has to take precedence over being their buddy.

But the relationship with your minor stepchildren was different from its inception. Hopefully, you started out as friends, and will maintain that friendship as their stepmother. If you didn't begin as friends, then you can only hope that friendship will start to grow as you spend more time together in the coming months and years. Although you may have had visions of a much closer relationship, being friends is usually the best you can hope for. Unfortunately, only a lucky few get to experience a true parent/child relationship with their stepchildren.

And don't even *think* about having them refer to you as *Mom*. They already have a mother—don't confuse the matter. Consider yourself fortunate if they'll at least call you by your first name. There are horror stories of stepmothers being called "it"—or worse! Don't push this issue. Friends call each other by their first name. When they call you by yours—smile.

Of course, there are all sorts of sordid scenarios when the whole stepparent/stepchild thing goes awry. And children often have emotional scars from their parents' divorce, which influence their behavior toward you. Again, there are professionals who specialize in this sort of challenge. You shouldn't hesitate to seek their assistance, if you feel you're not gaining ground in this area.

There are also other resources that focus on the issue of stepparenting, and some of those are listed at the back of this book. This survival guide doesn't attempt to determine the psychological requirements necessary to become a model stepparent, but rather simply allows the new stepmother the freedom to recognize her *feelings* about being one.

Kids are just kids, and both the stepparents and biological parents must remember that basic fact. But having said that, where is a struggling stepmother to go for moral support? Who can she vent to without fear of judgment or condemnation?

The sad truth is, probably not to most of her friends and family. After all, no one wants to hear a grown woman whine about how another woman's children have pushed her to her wit's end. And even though she needs to involve their father in the issue, she must tread lightly when voicing her opinion about his charges. They are blood of his blood, flesh of his flesh, and he will naturally defend them if he feels they are being attacked. So be sure your words and disposition don't assault them.

But do address the situation calmly and maturely with him. Your stepchildren's dislike of you isn't reason enough to allow them to freely ridicule, ignore, disobey, or disrespect you in any way. Your new husband must be with you on this. He needs to understand that loyalty to you does not mean he's being disloyal to his kids. In fact, only when he has his priorities properly aligned, will the children follow suit. If they realize that they can manipulate him and you—especially if they've figured out how to wedge themselves between you as a couple—it can spell disaster, not only for your new blended family, but for the remarriage itself.

In Matthew 19:5-6, Jesus instructs, *"...For this reason a man will leave his father and mother and be united to his wife, and the two will become one flesh. So they are no longer two, but one...."* (NIV) It's imperative that you both place your responsibilities to each other first—as mates for life. That's hard for many parents to swallow. However, contrary to what you may think, it doesn't mean casting off your parental instincts in favor of carefree immaturity. What it does mean is that you make a pact with each other that the children will never see you argue, especially about them. That you'll maintain a unified front, and whatever isn't agreed upon, will be worked out between you and your husband privately.

Minor children will usually come around, given enough time and nurturing, but not always. A lot depends on how much coaching they get at their mother's house. We've already mentioned that if the ex-wife supports your attempts at being good to her children, count your blessings. You're indeed one of the fortunate few. But if she's opposed to your very existence, you may never fully bridge the chasm between you and your minor stepchildren.

But there's one positive spin that stepparenting in a remarriage offers—the majority of children still reside with their mother full-time. That means you only have to endure their undesirable behaviors, every-other-weekend. Sound callous? So be it. This guide is about being real with yourself and your feelings. Don't start tiptoeing around the truth now. Your admittance doesn't make you a bad person—just a gut-level, honest one.

Your stepchildren have had a difficult time adjusting to your presence, and you have to confess that you breathe a sigh of relief when it's time for them to return to the ex-wife. That's not to say you won't be going to watch them play sports or act in a school play. But it does mean that Sunday evenings have become your favorite night of the week.

Hopefully, your relationship with your husband's children will improve to the point that you happily anticipate every other Friday evening, with more fervor than you'd ever dreaded it. But it may take years to arrive at that Utopia, if in fact, you ever get there.

Almost from the beginning, you arranged your own children's visitation schedule with their father, so that it'd correspond with your stepchildren's time with their mother. When this correlation in schedules worked, you reaped one of the only advantages that a remarried couple has over a first-time marriage—two whole days alone with each other, every other weekend! And you cherish this special gift of time to keep the fires of passion burning with your new mate. It almost reminds you of the pre-children years you had in your first marriage. Almost.

Spy Protégé

When Natalie married Michael, she immediately became the stepmother to his only child, a nine-year-old son, Joel. But Joel's visits with his dad had been sporadic during the three years since his parents' divorce. The boy's mother'd sought to punish Michael for leaving her, and had used the son they shared as her most potent weapon. She'd balked at the divorce decree's visitation schedule, or she simply hadn't been home when Michael'd tried to pick up his son. Several times, Michael'd had to have his attorney send her a warning letter, before she'd once again, begrudgingly allow her ex-husband his legal right to see his boy.

But almost immediately after the new couple's nuptials were spoken, Joel began visiting with the regularity that fiber-drink commercials promise. So why the sudden change? Had the ex-wife finally seen the error of her ways and encouraged her son's camaraderie with his dad? Had she realized the benefit of her son getting to know his new stepmother? Can you say F-A-T C-H-A-N-C-E?

Joel's mother had encouraged him to visit more often, all right. But it sure wasn't to bond with what she'd called the sleazy trash his father'd dragged home, like some stray dog. No, her motives were much more sinister than that. She'd instructed her nine-year-old to *spy*. What better way to find out the real scoop on what went on in that household, than to infiltrate the ranks with one of their own?

And Joel took his mission seriously. He was a natural. Quiet by nature, he could sneak up on conversations with the sure-footedness of a cat surprising its prey. Natalie couldn't say how many talks he'd overheard, since she was sure he'd never been caught listening to many of them.

One evening, she and Michael'd had an argument, and left Joel watching television while they went into their bedroom to discuss the matter privately. Mid-discussion, Michael suddenly stopped and pointed to the door. Natalie stealthily walked over and opened it. There stood Joel, his head cocked sideways where his ear had been pressed up against the wood.

Once, the ex-wife called and complained about something Natalie had said about her, although it'd never been said in front of Joel. In fact, Natalie believed she'd whispered that statement while lying in bed with Michael. She never did know how Joel had overheard her.

The boy obviously also told his mother every time he saw something new in the house. Several times the ex-wife took Michael back to court requesting more child support, based on his increased standard of living. But Natalie's income was the major reason for the upturn, and the court would only consider any raises Michael had received since the last decree. (At least one *next-wife* claims that in some states, the new wife's income *can* be considered in calculating support for the husband's children. If you're currently facing a similar circumstance, you might want to consult with an attorney to learn the laws in your state.)

Natalie had never envisioned having her privacy invaded as being part of her role as a stepmother. But her experience is all too common. The saddest part is, there's not a lot you can do about it, except watch what you say at all times while your stepchild is visiting.

Yet try to be as natural as possible, in spite of the tension you feel. After all, your husband's son or daughter is confused about his or her loyalties. But sadly, for most fathers, the child's commitment to the mother usually wins out. Blame genetic predisposition, matriarchal dominance, or sheer manipulation, but that's just normally the way the chips fall.

Adult Children—The Ultimate Paradox

But what if his children are grown and therefore, don't spend every-other-weekend with you and your husband? Does that mean you're home free? Far from it! Adult children can be even more destructive than minor ones! They're smarter, have a full range of resources at their disposal, and have learned lifelong, tried and true, maneuvers on how to push their dad's buttons.

Candace was ecstatic when Lance proposed.

47

He was handsome, intelligent, had risen to a respectable level in his career, and his children by a former marriage were in their twenties. She hurriedly told her best friend, Lila, the happy news.

Lila had been a *next-wife* herself for several years. Her eyes sparked with envy as she told Candace how fortunate she was that Lance's children were already grown. Candace would be spared the torture of being the every-other-weekend stepmom.

Candace agreed that it seemed like the perfect arrangement. She planned to have an adult friendship with all of his children, where she'd never have to be a "step" anything, but would simply be their father's wife. Both daughters and the son had left their mother's house years earlier, so Candace was sure she wouldn't pose a threat to them now at all.

Wrong again! When Lance married Candace, his son did little to conceal his apathy toward both his father and his new stepmother. However, he was just as unconcerned about his mom's post-divorce relationships. Rather than face the uncomfortable reality that his parents were never going to reconcile, this young man refused to acknowledge either parent. And his preoccupation with his budding career, was the perfect excuse not to invest any more time and energy into the mess their divorce had made of the family.

The youngest daughter threw a bona fide tantrum that rivaled any toddler's. She demanded that her father abide by her "rules" of not including Candace in their social functions, or she'd stop all contact with him. She clung to her mother like a fly on doo-doo, and the ex spurred on this childish scheme. Unfortunately, the relationship between Lance and both of these children remains severed years later.

The remaining daughter has struggled to maintain some semblance of a relationship with her father. However, she's vacillated between love for her dad, and loyalty to her mom and sister.

Truly, no one has been the winner in the above scenario. But fortunately, the remarriage between Candace and Lance has not been harmed by the antics of these adult children. They have held tightly to one another as they've weathered these storms. Lance knew that he could not allow his grown children to emotionally blackmail him into forsaking Candace, and she's fortunate that he's been insightful about their behavior. (Check the resource section at the back of this guide for an excellent book on emotional blackmail.)

If his adult children ever want a closer relationship with him, Lance will be ready and willing to be there for them. But not with the conditions they placed on his love. Lance and Candace are a package deal—the two have become one. And he knows that if he's ever able to have the kind of relationship he desires to have with his adult children, it will be based on mutual love and respect, and not on manipulation and contrived betrayals.

Another father in Lance's position, might give in to the demands of his grown children. Perhaps he's riddled with guilt over the demise of his first marriage, even though it'd died after the children were raised. Or maybe he's in denial that the bundles of joy he'd sired and nurtured, have grown to be self-centered and manipulative adults.

He may even subconsciously try to *buy* a relationship with them. His outrageously generous gifts—which the children firmly expect and feel entitled to—have protected them from the pain of learning how to survive on their own. He's paid them off with the regularity of a mortgage payment, without ever gaining equity in a *real* relationship with them. He's never known true compassion from his little darlings, or what it feels like for them to acknowledge that he's a living, breathing, human being, with wants and desires of his own.

He's settled instead for being their wallet. And if their father is the wallet, then his *next-wife* must be the pickpocket, the thief, the gold-digger. And it's *their* gold. They aren't about to watch a strange woman (and they believe you are *very* strange) get her hands on their inheritance! Meanwhile, their mother cheers them on from the sidelines, and even occasionally jumps into the ring with them.

Parenting is tough enough for original parents. It's even more difficult for stepmothers. So, regardless of where you find yourself in this "step" process, expect that you'll get out of step occasionally. Be prepared for getting your toes stepped on from time to time. But don't let it throw you. Just take a deep breath and keep on trying. For just as in original parenting, the rewards of successful stepparenting are well worth a few bruised toes along the way.

Ex-Wives and Ex-Lives:

Chapter Five:

Picture This!

Survival Ex-ism #5

EXpose

Truth is in perception
All is revealed in time,
So *expose* the fallacy;
The picture-perfect kind.

You saw his ex-wife's grinning mug immediately. And there, directly behind her with his hand on her shoulder, was your new husband. An old family portrait greeted you as your husband's grandmother opened her door. You actually hesitated to enter, as if the elderly woman was beckoning you to step back into a bygone era, from which you'd never escape.

But with a slight nudge from your husband, you did get your feet to move forward. You even managed a hug for his grandmother right on cue, when he introduced you as his new wife. But you could feel his ex-wife's presence as you entered the house, and could've sworn her eyes followed you down the hallway. You shivered, and tried to shake off the weight that pressed in on your heart.

"It's just a picture," you silently consoled yourself, "Just one moment frozen in time." And although you'd noticed the playful upturn of his lips, you'd dismissed it as merely a pose, staged for the camera's sake. The sparkle of genuine joy had never made it to his eyes. No, your husband couldn't have been happy when that picture was taken.

There were more in the living room. Snapshots dotted the furniture landscape like morning flowers in a Spring meadow. Your new husband with his children. Your new husband with his ex-wife. Your new husband and his ex-wife and your new grandma-in-law.

You pleadingly looked to your husband for reassurance, but he just impishly grinned and shrugged his shoulders as if to say, "She's old. Let it go."

You'd heard that elderly people have difficulty accepting change. Even your own grandparents still used a television with rabbit ears, and thought the VCR was state-of-the-art technology. Yet you'd never experienced a time-warp like the one you were witnessing now.

But you hadn't seen anything compared to what you were about to hear. So when Grandma started talking, you tried valiantly to tone her out. You even chose to stare mindlessly at those pictures, rather than subject yourself to her verbal assaults.

Did she really just ask your husband how his ex-wife was, and tearfully admitted how much she missed her? Of course, Grandma didn't mention that the woman she was referring to was her grandson's ex, but tenderly spoke her name, as if savoring the taste of expensive chocolate.

Your husband answered that she was fine, and tried to change the subject to the new house the two of you had purchased. But Grandma just exclaimed what a beautiful house he'd had with his ex-wife, and what a shame it'd been for them to sell it.

He tried again to bring you into the conversation, remarking on your successful catering business. But she wasn't about to take the bait. She was only reminded how crafty his ex-wife had been, and got up to retrieve a scrapbook as proof. It showed them all—including Grandma—on a vacation together. In the backdrop of crystal blue skies, white sands were littered with scantily-clad bodies. In one shot, your bare-chested husband embraced his ex-wife, with both kids making faces at the camera.

Great! That's just what you wanted to see— his ex-wife looking decent in a bikini (although she really should've tried to burn off those thighs!) skin-to-skin with the man you now called your husband. And there sat Grandma under the shade of her umbrella, fully dressed and grinning like a baby about to pass gas.

When your visit was finally (and mercifully) over, you felt as if you'd been pummeled by a champion boxer. You were dizzy from holding your breath so long, and your tongue resembled raw hamburger where you'd been biting it.

But your husband wrapped his arm around your waist as you walked to the car, and whispered his love for you as he opened the door. You exhaled slowly. At last you could relax, comforted by assurances of his dedication to you—his wife.

This scenario has been played out in numerous *next-wives* lives with some variation. Of course, his grandmother may not have been the culprit. It could have been his mother, sister, uncle, cousin—any family member. And one person may not have done it all. Perhaps the behavior had been spread across a variety of his relatives or former acquaintances. And as we'll see below, it could even go beyond lifeless pictures and mindless comments.

In-laws or Outlaws?

When Hannah married Charles, she discovered that his family was still very friendly with his ex-wife. They had loved her dearly, and saw no reason why the family should divorce her just because Charles had. This is understandable in itself. However, this clan took that principle to an extreme.

The first Thanksgiving Hannah and Charles celebrated as a couple, they were invited to Charles' brother's house for dinner. But as they stepped inside, they were accosted with more than the aroma of plum pudding and turkey. Hannah smelled a rat when his ex-wife greeted them at the door. The family had included her in their holiday celebration, as they'd done for the previous fifteen years, as if nothing had changed at all. And his ex-wife had accepted their invitation with the knowledge that her ex-husband and his new wife would also be there. Hannah and Charles had not been offered the same courtesy of seeing the guest list in advance.

This routine repeated itself for the Christmas gathering, the annual Easter egg hunt, birthdays, and other family celebrations. Charles' brother even made a joke that since the ex-wife had been his in-law for so long, maybe Hannah could be his *outlaw*. Hannah hadn't found the comment amusing.

So how can a *next-wife* survive such blatant animosity toward her? A lot depends on how close your new husband is to his family to begin with, and how clearly he sees that the situation is demoralizing and disrespectful to you. If he has this insight, then it's his responsibility to talk with his family members privately, and explain that their behavior won't be tolerated in the future. They may test him, and relationships may be strained temporarily. But if he stands his ground, eventually they'll understand that he meant what he said. He'll refuse to go to any more family functions until he's assured that they'll respect his new wife, by not inviting his former one.

However, if he doesn't comprehend the severity of the situation, it doesn't look good for you. You could refuse to go with him, and risk spending holidays alone. Of course, that would also build resentment and probably spell disaster for your remarriage.

Which is exactly what happened with Hannah

and Charles. He didn't understand why his ex-wife's presence bothered Hannah so much. When she complained to him, he accused her of being jealous and controlling.

When the couple had been married almost three years, Hannah's parents announced their intent to visit from another state on Easter. However, Charles' family always gathered at his aunt's house for an Easter egg hunt. When Hannah told her parents about their previous plans, they happily agreed to go with them. They believed it would be a nice opportunity to get to know Charles' side of the family better.

But his aunt refused to allow them to attend, and justified her rudeness by using the *immediate family only* excuse. Naturally, this infuriated Hannah, and she refused to go without her parents.

Charles' children had been looking forward to the event, though, and he didn't want to disappoint them. Hannah offered to orchestrate their own Easter egg hunt, but he wouldn't hear of it. After all, they'd *always* had the hunt at his aunt's house. It was tradition.

So Charles and his children spent Easter with his extended family. Hannah and her parents bought takeout chicken and spent the day at home. A week later, Hannah filed for divorce. She didn't even cry at the dissolution of her remarriage, and of seeing the hopes and dreams she'd had for a wonderful future with Charles disintegrate. His ultimate betrayal of her love and trust by repeatedly choosing his extended family over her, had turned her heart to an impenetrable stone.

Perhaps their situation had been compounded by the fact that his family had rejected her parents. Regardless, the consequences of Charles' misplaced priorities, were spelled out loud and clear when he was served with the divorce papers.

A Family Affair

Leah and George encountered quite another type of family togetherness—too much of it. They visited George's father and his new wife, Hazel, often, and enjoyed going on camping trips with them. Technically, Hazel was George's stepmother, but she'd married his father later in life, so George had never known her in that capacity.

Usually, Hazel's grown daughter, Brenda, was also present. Brenda was a couple of years older than Leah, but she still lived with her mother (Hazel) and George's father, so Leah thought nothing of her being included in their visits.

Unfortunately, Leah and George divorced after only a couple of years of remarriage. This in itself was tragic enough. But to add insult to injury, George hooked up with Brenda, even before his divorce from Leah was final. Only weeks after the decree was issued, he married his sister! Granted,

61

it was his stepsister, and not one that he'd grown up with. Nevertheless, in the five years since his dad had married her mom, she'd been the "sister" of the family.

It left Leah scarred and distrustful. Had Charles and Brenda been having an affair under her nose? She'd never know for sure. She searched her mind for signs of indiscretion, and although she remembered hugging and well-wishing between them, she'd never suspected that George had felt anything more than brotherly love toward his stepsister. In her wildest nightmares, she'd never have believed that the "other woman" would turn out to be a family member! It reminded her of a sick redneck joke about a branchless family tree, and it left her nauseous.

Picture Perfect?

Now to address those irritating past family photos you stumbled upon while cleaning out the bedroom closet. Not *your* pictures. Yours are sealed in a box and stored away from sight and inadvertent discovery. No, these are his pictures—of her and his life before you.

Should you demand that he dispose of them? Should you sneak them out in the garbage without his knowledge? By the time he missed them, there'd be no proof of how they'd disappeared. The most likely scenario would be that they'd never made it to the new house at all, but had gotten misplaced during your move there. Everyone knows that moving buries keepsakes into a deep abyss, never to be seen again. Like your favorite sweater that vanished between your old home and the new one.

But your sense of fair play won't allow you to take the easy road. You can't simply dispose of the proof you hold in your hand of his past life. No, you'll have to deal with this like the mature adult you are. And you are a mature adult, regardless of the conflicting emotions you're having at the moment.

The right thing to do is to leave his memories alone. As long as he's not pulling them out reminiscing on a regular basis—and especially in your presence—then he's entitled to keep whatever mementos of his past that he desires. Of course, if he goes so far as to display a picture of his ex-wife, or an old family portrait where you or any visitor could see, then you have more troubles than the mere picture! He's obviously not come to terms with the past, and may need professional counseling to learn how to do so.

Remember, you are equally entitled to keep the pictures from your past. But afford your new husband the same respect you require, and don't flaunt them in his face. The best solution is for you both to separate them into three groups: one you'll give to the children for their memories; one you want to keep; and one for the trash. Box up the keepers, and store them out of sight.

Karla discovered too late that her new husband, Sam, had a serious issue when it came to letting bygones be bygones. She returned home from work one evening and discovered a huge portrait of Sam's former family hanging over their bed. Her husband's ex-wife's image was center-stage in the one room that should've been totally off-limits. Even worse, the picture included Sam's three-year-old daughter, who'd tragically died years earlier from a rare childhood disease.

Naturally, Karla was distressed at having this portrait hanging over her head at night, but Sam refused to take it down or to move it to another room. Ultimately, she discovered that Sam suffered from more than just nostalgia. His behavior ran the gamut from bizarre (cursing at her more prolifically than a Tourette's Syndrome sufferer, or talking out loud to his dead daughter), to the dangerous (threatening to harm himself, and to take Karla with him to join his little girl).

That picture spoke of something much more ominous than just a harmless image in a frame. It foretold of Sam's mental illness, which had initially been triggered by the loss of his child. The same child that had been conceived out of wedlock before marrying his ex-wife, and the one he'd tried unsuccessfully to convince his ex to abort.

Sam had managed to conceal his illness in the guise of healthy grief, that would be expected of any caring father. But then he and Karla had begun making plans to have a baby together. Karla suspected that Sam perceived the new child would replace his deceased daughter, and the guilt had finally broken him. Regardless, he'd plummeted over the edge of reality, and had scared her beyond consolation. She packed her things and moved out, the faces in the picture taunting her as she walked away.

Strictly speaking, a picture is just a piece of paper where a chemical has produced an image. It has no life of its own, unless the possessor of it determines that it does. Someday, both of you may wish to look at those old pictures again and reminisce, or perhaps not. Either way, you'll have the choice at that time.

However, those reminders of your past truly have no place in your current life or remarriage. Granted, neither you nor your new husband, just appeared on this earth at the moment of your meeting. You each lived a life—good or bad, happy or sad—before the other one came onto the scene.

But what was before, is gone forever. Have a portrait taken of your new family to capture your own moment in time together. And remember, it's the pictures imprinted in your heart and mind that really matter. Paper photos fade with age, but memories can last a lifetime.

Ex-Wives and Ex-Lives:

Chapter Six:

The Name Game

Survival Ex-ism #6

EXcuse

To forgive is divine,
That ideal is so high,
Still, you must *excuse* him;
For he's just a man—**Sigh!**

The lights are low. Romantic music is playing softly in the background. The fire in the hearth burns only slightly hotter than you and your new husband, as you embrace on the floor in front of it. He murmurs sweet somethings in your ear...and you bolt upright. One "something" he just whispered was his ex-wife's name!

You switch on the light, and its starkness floods your husband's suddenly pale face. He stares at you with the disbelief of an animal caught in the glare of headlights. It's as if his life flashes before his eyes. He can't even defend himself. He's lying there on the floor, as exposed emotionally as he is physically. And as good as dead.

The sucker punch of his careless comment has left you reeling, and for a moment, you don't know what hit you. Then your adrenaline courses through your veins, demanding that you fight or flee. But who is your opponent? Your husband? Or the intruder who masqueraded as him, only to stab you in the heart with the blade of that woman's name?

And if you fled instead, where could you hide?

Is there a place where the remembrance of that spoken name won't infiltrate? Can you ever be sheltered from what he just said in the heat of passion, or will its echo taunt you forever?

You want to scream, but when you open your mouth, it remains cavernous and silent. You feel the familiar weight of grief pressing against your heart and lungs, and expect the tears to spill over the dam of your emotions. Yet your eyes are distant and removed, and remain dry and unblinking. And not even one single sob escapes from your still-open mouth.

When your husband realizes that you're frozen in shock, and that there are no weapons of convenience nearby, he jumps up to comfort you. He wraps his arms around you and apologizes profusely. He begs you to forgive him and promises that it'll never happen again. He swears that it was just a slip of the tongue and meant nothing. He knew exactly whom he was making love to. It was you, just you, and would always be *only* you. He offers to cut out his tongue—which seemingly acted of its own volition—if that sacrifice would prove his love is true.

Your spirit watches the scenario from somewhere high in the corner of the room. A part of you has died. Gone is that innocent woman who'd found her Prince Charming. The one who'd thrown herself into her lover/husband's arms with reckless abandon, secure in his desire for her. Only her.

You see his lips move, but the sound limps behind them as if in a poorly dubbed movie. Are those tears in his eyes? Funny, but you're numb now to feeling anything at all.

Yet a part of you wants to feel sorry for him. After all, you have an ex-husband. What if you'd been the one to utter his name at such an intimate moment?

But your anger flares at the thought of it. You could consider "what if" scenarios all day long. The truth of the matter is that you've never made such a serious blunder, and doubt that you ever would. No, you can't help but believe that if your husband had truly been in the moment with you, instead of reliving some past experience, he would never have committed such a travesty.

You want to punish him. You want to console him. You want to banish him from your life forever. You want to get back on the floor and finish what the two of you'd started earlier. You're dizzy from the conflicting emotions, and watch as your husband gently leads your swaying body over to the sofa to sit down.

Suddenly, you realize that you are also naked, your body exposed to the scrutiny of the man who just called you by another woman's name. For reasons you don't fully understand, you feel violated. You stand up with all the pride you can muster, and announce that you need some time alone. You hold your head high as you walk unsteadily to the bathroom, where a scalding hot tub will soon beckon.

Within minutes, you sink chin-high into the scented water, the reflections of candles burning along its edges, and breathe a sigh of release. Only now will you at last allow yourself to cry.

Experts claim that men are hard-wired differently than women. They function from routine, memory, even carrying on whole conversations seemingly by rote. Whereas women are more deliberate and intentional, men click into autopilot and hop on.

Maybe so. But that doesn't minimize the pain his careless automatic reference to his ex-wife caused you, his *next-wife*. And yet, what choice do you have but to forgive him? You meant your vow of sticking together through better or worse. You just never imagined how suddenly and completely that "worse part" would engulf you.

You're aware that try as he might, he can't unsay words already said. All he can do is plead for mercy. And in your heart, you know you have to give that to him.

However, beware if he doesn't ask for forgiveness, but instead blames you for being petty and too sensitive! His callousness may be indicative of more than just temporary defensiveness. It could be a sign of worse things to come—verbal or emotional abuse—where he puts you down as a quick fix to his own insecurities.

Ultimately, after you've endured the blow of

being called her name, you must allow the soothing balm of forgiveness to heal the hurt and restore your trust in your husband's love. And don't be surprised if he isn't even more attentive and loving than ever before, now that his senses will be in heightened awareness of *you.* After all, he's not about to press his luck by committing that *almost* unpardonable sin again!

Social Suicide

The above scenario was at least a private affair between husband and wife. But what if the new husband's *faux pas* was aired as publicly as if on a sordid afternoon talk show?

Delores and Mitch were remarried newlyweds. As is common with many new next-wives, Delores was anxious to be accepted by Mitch's friends and acquaintances. This desire was compounded by the fact that when she married Mitch, Delores had relocated from another town, so she basically had no friends of her own yet.

But she was particularly nervous about meeting his coworkers at the annual Christmas party. Mitch had worked for the same company for years, including when he'd been married before, so most of his peers had known his ex-wife. It was always worse for Delores when she was aware that she was meeting associates of Mitch's ex.

The party was going well, though, until Myles and Gwen came up to speak to Mitch. Things headed south in a hurry when he introduced his new wife, by regurgitating his ex-wife's name.

But Delores didn't miss a beat. She smiled sweetly and extended her hand to Gwen first (whom she swore was smirking) and then to Myles, She refused to acknowledge her husband's blunder, especially since she'd been told that Myles and Gwen still regularly socialized with Mitch's ex.

After a few minutes, Mitch and Delores excused themselves, and Delores informed her husband that the party was over. They left soon afterward.

Privately, visions taunted Delores of Gwen rushing home to call Mitch's ex. She could almost hear the echo of the two women's laughter, at how Mitch apparently hadn't gotten over his former spouse, after all.

So what's a *next-wife* to do? Again, the situation can't be rewound and the offensive name edited out. Mitch will probably chalk it up to being just an unfortunate mental lapse, and forget about it. But it may forever languish in Delores' memory. Yet her forgiveness of him is ultimately the only way to clear the path, as they trudge forward in their relationship.

The same logic applies here as in the first example. Although Mitch's transgression wasn't during the heat of passion, perhaps it was even more damaging because it was done publicly. Delores will need to reign in those images of humiliation that'd mocked her, and get back to what really matters— her remarriage to Mitch. And again, Mitch needs to own the part he played in embarrassing his new wife, albeit unintentionally. Then, the newly remarried couple needs to put it behind them and go on.

In the grand scheme of things, does it really matter what his ex thinks of you? Or even former friends, for that matter? What's much more important is that you and your new husband are able to overcome uncomfortable and hurtful situations like these. Your remarriage will not only survive, but grow stronger in the process. Both of you need to understand that past baggage will show up on your doorstep at the most unexpected and inopportune times. That doesn't mean you have to open it and wallow in its contents. Just zip it up and send it back.

Because, unlikely as it seems to you now, someday it may be *you* that accidentally spills out a past name. Or perhaps you'll recount a fond memory with your new husband of your vacation in Maui, only to realize too late that you've never been there together. That was another time and another husband. And your new husband will be all too aware that the two of you have never been on that particular vacation.

Although time together in your remarriage will help alleviate some of these slipups, the best remedy is for your husband to replace the old name, by using yours often (he should speak your *actual name*—not Honey, or Bunny, or Pumpkin-Pie) in order to hard-wire it in for future reference.

And just as with the picture scenarios talked about in a previous chapter, make your own memories together. Rewrite over the old data with new. The former images can still be extracted purposefully, if desired, but the new memories and the newest name—yours—will be the first and most spontaneous generated. It's called top of the mind awareness, and marketing professionals have been using it for years to elicit spur-of-the-moment buying decisions. It'll work in your relationship too, given a little attention to detail and time.

And one more note. You may want to practice keeping your eyes open during intimate moments for a while. Gaze lovingly at your husband as he tenderly whispers the verbal equivalent of pure gold— the sound of your name on the lips of your lover.

Chapter Seven:

Help Me!
I'm Living Another
Woman's Life!

Survival Ex-ism #7

EXude

You've wasted much energy
Comparing yourself to her,
It's time to *exude* the essence of you;
Strong, beautiful, and sure.

Walls that talk. A pervasive *presence* that walks the halls, wandering between rooms. Eyes that hover around the dinner table, and even worse, over the master bed. A haunted house? Not by the usual definition, but haunted nevertheless. You see, you live in *her* house.

Oh, your new husband explained how it was always him who'd loved the house. Even though he and his ex built it together, and spent ten years of their married life there, she hadn't put up any fight at all when she'd moved out.

But it was home to him. Besides, his children have never lived anywhere else. Why should they be put through the turmoil of changing neighborhoods, friends, and schools, by moving? So you agreed to dwell in this residence of memories. And lived to regret it. Every single day.

Innocently, you'd anticipated creating your dream life with your new husband. You'd never considered that perhaps a new location, was one prerequisite to accomplishing that goal. But this oversight slapped you in the face the first morning you woke up in "her" bedroom. It was as if you stepped into her slippers, and shuffled into their twelfth year of marriage. You felt as if you were the understudy in her life's play, and wondered if your new husband even noticed that a different face greeted him with the sun.

So you'd set out to make a name—and place—for yourself as best you could. At first, you thought if you painted the walls a different color, it would erase her presence. But that wasn't enough. Next, you tried remodeling the kitchen—new cabinets, a different color of countertop, the latest in appliance fashions, new tile and wallpaper. That should've done it. But it didn't.

A woman often spends a lot of time in the kitchen, and as such, it reflects her own personality. But when you were finished with this project, all you saw was a showroom display that still wasn't what *you* would've created, had you designed it originally. Even though everything in the room was new, it remained connected to the rest of the house that *she* had built. (And speaking of building a house...you've begun to resent the fact that he'd thought she was worthy of her very own, brand new home, while you've had to settle for her seconds.)

Finally, you added on a sun room, a special niche carved out just for you. You'd dreamed of curling up in a cushioned chaise lounge, the sunlight embracing you in warmth, with the latest best-seller in your hand—a temporary ticket to another time and place. Unfortunately, it didn't take long before the stark reality hit you that even this taste of Eden, was still an appendage to the rest of *her* house.

And no matter how creative you were, you just couldn't conquer the master bedroom. Your new husband at least had the decency to move his and his ex-wife's bedroom suite into the guest room, and the two of you bought a new bed together. Unfortunately, the effort was comparable to using a lawn sprinkler to douse a five-alarm blaze. Yet if you *haven't* gotten rid of the old furniture, you must have the tolerance level of a saint! Either that, or your self-esteem is so low that you don't think you deserve even your own bed.

You've tried everything imaginable, and still you've felt like an intruder in what was supposed to be your home. So how can a *next-wife* survive the prison of those walls?

That depends on your particular circumstances. Janet and Tom experienced a similar situation as the scenario just described. But Tom was a farmer, and therefore, couldn't just pick up and move elsewhere. Janet had no choice but to stick it out and make the best of her situation.

When her efforts failed to convince Tom to build another house in a different location on their land, she got him to do the next best thing—they added on several rooms and a whole second story! By the time Janet was finished, the core that had been his house (which incidentally, she'd already completely remodeled) was almost obliterated by the new additions. There was no mistaking it for the same abode. She had successfully extracted the ex-wife's memories from what was now truly *Janet's* and Tom's home.

But what if the only justification for living in the ex-wife's house is that your new husband likes it, or moving would disrupt the children's lives? Let's look at these reasons one at a time.

The Comfort Crisis

What is your new husband thinking? Hasn't anyone explained to him that the nesting impulse is instinctual to a woman? And a home is her nest, the safe place she provides for her family. But if she doesn't feel safe there herself, that insecurity will permeate the remarriage relationship, as well as that of the new blended family.

Every woman deserves her own choice in living accommodations. It should not be delegated to her by her husband, and especially not by his ex-wife! Remarriage is tough enough without bringing in unnecessary encumbrances, such as a house that he'd shared with another woman. If your husband loves you like you hope he does, your happiness together needs to come first. The choice of living quarters should be mutually acceptable, not just what *he* feels most comfortable with.

As mentioned earlier, no amount of redecorating or remodeling (short of almost totally rebuilding) will satisfy the new wife that this house is indeed, her home. In bygone eras, a woman used the home—usually the only means she had available to her—as her competitive edge against other women who might have their sights set on her husband. This antiquated woman saw to it that her home was inviting and comfortable, a place where her husband would be grateful to come to night after night. She had to ensure that her man would indeed bring back the bacon he'd been out in the world making all day. Survival of her bloodline depended on him returning to the nest to care for her offspring.

Fortunately, times have changed and women no longer depend on men to this extreme. However, the innate nesting instinct remains. Although it's stronger in some women than with others, to deny its existence is to deny the same basic drive that catapults a mother to defend her young against perceived threats. Both nesting and protecting are usually done without conscious thought. That's part of the definition of instinct. And instinct can't be overcome by simply *willing* yourself not to have it.

Don't be a martyr here! You don't have anything to prove by agreeing to live in *her* house, but you risk losing everything! This can't be emphasized enough. If you compromise on this issue, you *will* regret it. Period.

Children's Choice

Your new husband explained how his children were still reeling from his divorce from their mother, and now they'd have to accept that their dad had a new wife. He couldn't also force them to move from the only home they'd ever known. His pleading eyes begged you to understand his plight, and your heart melted.

But do you have children from a former marriage? Are they moving into your new husband's house? Will that cause them to change schools, make new friends, etc.? So why the double standard?

Perhaps your new love is trying to appease his guilt for having caused his own children the pain of a "broken" home in the first place. Maybe if they're allowed to remain in the same structure they've grown up in, it'll almost be as if their original home had never split at all.

It doesn't work. Staying in the same house won't take away all of the pain they've experienced from their parents' divorce. In fact, it may do just the opposite. Seeing another woman living in their mother's former home, can be like leaving a splinter in a wound to fester. It's much better to endure the temporary pain of removing the reminder, in the interest of complete future healing.

Children are resilient. They may not like moving at first, but they'll adjust. Life is full of changes. The best gift to give children, is to teach them how to adapt to these inevitable reorganizations, instead of pretending they'll never have to face them.

And have you really given any thought to how his children will react when they sprint down to the breakfast table—the same table where their mother greeted them for years—only to find you, their new stepmother, standing in your bathrobe in *her* kitchen? Don't be fooled. His children will continue to feel their mother's presence in the house where they all used to live as a family.

If your own children are moving in with you as well, his children may resent having their "territory" encroached upon by these stepsiblings. Beginning on new ground is the only way to ensure that everyone is on equal footing. No one will have already homesteaded the biggest bedroom, or the one with the bay windows, or the room with the most privacy. And your stepdaughter won't resent you for adding your personal touch to the living room, because she won't have helped her mother decorate it before her parents divorced.

Dump the former house! What is lost will be more than compensated for, by the peace attained from giving your new life together a fighting chance.

Exorcise those old memories by refusing to let them languish at the death scene of his former marriage. You wouldn't expect your new blended family to live there had an actual murder occurred, would you?

Centuries ago, punishment for death penalty offenses included strapping a corpse onto the back of the condemned man. Death was slowly and agonizingly transferred to the living person, by the rotting and disease-infested flesh of the dead one. And by the time it finally came, the Grim Reaper was actually welcomed. The inescapable torture of dragging around death as a constant companion, had driven the condemned man to insanity, long before his body succumbed to its inevitable physical demise.

Don't do this to the health and life of your new union! Bury the reminders of past relationships in the tombs of former dwellings, and move on. Your remarriage deserves a life—*and a house*—of its own.

Chapter Eight:

Coming Out

Survival Ex-ism #8

EXclaim

You'll shout it from the mountain
Or whisper it in the night,
But however you *exclaim* the truth;
It is your human right.

For centuries, the *next-wife* has been accused of being the other woman. She's epitomized the stereotypical wicked stepmother, while her predecessor has continued to shine like a brand new penny. After all, the ex has lost her husband, and now, every-other-weekend, her children will be forced to cavort with the likes of their father's *next-wife*. She has a right to act like a...woman scorned.

So you're expected to be understanding and tolerant of her—friendly even—without displaying a sliver of irritation at her antics. And should you stray from this unrealistic ideal, you're the one accused of being petty.

In a society where anything goes and alternative lifestyles are embraced, it seems the only remaining taboo is your attitude toward his ex-wife. You don't like her. There, you've said it. And your lips didn't roll up like window shades to your eyebrows, from breaking the curse of hypocritical silence.

Actually, your dislike of her is even stronger. There's but a thin line between hate and love, and there's never been any risk of you wasting any love on her. But you refuse to expend your valuable time by investing in an emotion as strong as hate, so you'll settle for dislike.

But who can you share these honest emotions with? Certainly your new husband is already aware of them, yet undoubtedly, doesn't want to hear about it—again. You can't tell his children just how low-down you think their mother is, and you wouldn't expose this side of your usual good nature to your own children, either. After all, you've taught them the Biblical principle of loving their enemies. Would they ever respect you again if they knew the truth?

So you hold it in. You smile sweetly whenever you have to face the ex, and are polite and engaging as you inquire how she is. But you already know how she is, regardless of what she tries to portray. She really thinks she has you fooled, and it just eats you up that you can't expose her charades publicly. *Sigh*

Talk About Trouble!

Laura came home one day to discover her husband, Elliott, talking on the phone to his ex-wife. He'd kicked back in his chair, and his feet were propped up on the desk of their home office. He nearly fell backward when Laura's early arrival surprised him. He abruptly ended the conversation.

He volunteered that he'd been talking to his ex, even though Laura already knew that without his confession. There's something about how a man's countenance changes when the ex-wife is near, even via the phone lines. The look that steals across his face may be pleasure, or perhaps, it's pure torture. But either way, the *next-wife* can always detect the presence of her predecessor. Always.

Elliott explained that his ex had called to ask him some questions about his new wife. He had only been remarried a few months, and his ex thought she deserved to know more about the woman who would be around her eleven-year old daughter, during Elliott's scheduled visits.

Initially, that appeared to be a valid request. Here was a mother, concerned about the safety and well-being of her child. She certainly had a right to know what kind of character the *next-wife* possessed. It was her motherly responsibility to ensure that her daughter would be accepted and not mistreated. And if that had indeed been her motive, this scenario never would've made it into the pages of this survival guide.

But Laura quickly saw through the ex-wife's ruse, when Elliott went on to relay parts of the conversation. The ex hadn't asked the obvious questions of, "Has she ever been accused of abuse?" Or, "Does she have a propensity for violence?" Or even, "What's her view on spanking?"

Instead, she'd lamented what an awful

reputation the *next-wife* had, and wanted to know if the rumors were true that she'd secretly dated Elliott's best friend, before she'd met Elliott. Laura suspected the ex had hoped this news would shock him back into his senses, and catapult him into getting a quickie divorce.

Laura was livid! What did her former dating habits have to do with treating her new stepdaughter graciously? The obvious answer was *nothing*. But the ex-wife had used the guise of being a good mother to administer shock therapy to Elliott, as well as to engage in plain old gossip. And even worse, Laura's new husband admitted to entertaining his ex-wife's sham for thirty minutes before Laura arrived.

So how did Laura handle this precarious situation? She threw the proverbial fit! How could her husband betray her like that? How could he listen to another woman slam his wife's character, without defending her?

According to Elliott, he had defended her, but that plea was lost on Laura. As far as she was concerned, when he realized that his ex's worry for their child had been fabricated as a way to attack his new wife, he should've refused to play along and hung up.

Of course, Laura was reacting from the assumption that Elliott *recognized* what his ex-wife was up to. Unfortunately, it's not unusual for a man to have lived years with his former spouse, suffered at her hand during an ugly divorce, and yet his naiveté about her character survived, relatively unscathed. Go figure.

A friend counseled Laura that Elliott had a right to talk to anyone he chose to, about anyone he pleased. This advice was fine, if you're looking at the letter of the law. But if you take in the whole picture, the safety net of the remarital relationship had been stretched to its limits. Both husband and *next-wife* should feel secure that confidences will be protected and kept private. Elliott should have refused to discuss Laura's dating past with anyone—especially his ex-wife. Frankly, Laura's former social life was none of the ex's business, and her intent to harm Laura and her relationship with Elliott, should have been obvious. Even to an ex-husband.

Defensively, Laura felt entitled to point out the ex's myriad personality defects to Elliott, but to her surprise, he became angry with *Laura*. He accused her of making a big deal over nothing, and justified his right to have a conversation with his ex about their daughter.

It would seem that the ex-wife was the only woman in this triad that was able to speak her mind freely. She'd voiced her utter repulsion at Elliott's choice in a new mate, and when she hung up the phone, Laura was certain it was with the triumphant look and smug satisfaction of a job well done.

Puppeteer Extraordinaire

Jessica and Kyle had been married only a short while, when Jessica began to sense a strange sensation. It was as if the impulses that controlled her arms, legs, and mouth, were being prompted by an outside source. But her mind was clear and focused, and she resisted the attempt to deny her unalienable right to her own free will.

It'd all started with a phone call. Kyle's ex-wife had called him at work (a habit that unnerved Jessica) to explain that when their daughter'd returned from her scheduled visit the previous week, she'd complained that Jessica had denied her a second cookie. Kyle's ex was appalled at Jessica's blatant disregard for who was—or was not—the child's mother. She instructed Kyle that if their little angel wanted a second cookie, it was not up to Jessica to overrule her.

Of course, Kyle's daughter had failed to mention that this second-cookie request had been made a mere thirty minutes before dinner. And Kyle hadn't voiced that detail, either. He simply listened and said he'd relay the information to his wife. Which he did.

Jessica was incensed! How dare that woman try to reach into her home and strong-arm her into bowing to the wiles of *any* child!

But the ex wasn't finished with her maneuvers yet. She contacted Kyle again (of course she called him at work!) to tell him to tell Jessica to stop discussing her with other people. *What?* That's what she said. Apparently, someone had mentioned the ex-wife to Jessica, and her reply wasn't complimentary. That person rushed to tell the ex what Jessica had said and...you get the picture. Pure childishness, which is particularly ugly when displayed by adults.

Obviously, Kyle's ex-wife's need to control was, well...out of control. Did she *really* think she could dictate what Jessica said and to whom? Jessica threatened to call the ex and give her a piece of her mind, but then thought better of it. What would such a display of hostility solve? It would just prove that the ex had pushed one of her emotional buttons. Jessica quickly came to her senses and ignored the ex's failed coup. After all, no one could control her without her consent, and she wasn't giving it.

The Ultimate Betrayal

Returning to Laura and Elliott once more, there is a sad postscript to their situation. When Elliott's ex-wife realized that her attempt had failed to wreak havoc between Elliott and Laura, she played her trump card. And this time, she succeeded in causing a permanent rift between Laura and the child. However, even that was not enough for her. She used her influence with the daughter she and

Elliott shared, to turn the girl against him, too.

Elliott was devastated. This was his only daughter—his only child—and he loved her dearly. Yet the girl's mother had custody, and Elliott's visitations were the typical every other weekend schedule. How could he possibly win back his daughter's affections during those few days, when she was influenced by her mother the rest of the time?

How had the ex succeeded at something so drastic? She strummed her daughter's strings of loyalty, that's how. Her constant derogatory remarks about Laura and Elliott eventually took root. The mother manipulated the child's affections so that her daughter's love for her dad, meant disloyalty to her mom. She told her that her daddy had a new family now that didn't include her. And the icing on the child's guilt cake was when her mother lamented that her daughter was all she had. Visiting her father meant her mom would be left all alone.

A heavy load to carry for anyone, especially a confused eleven-year-old child.

Are you still wondering why a *next-wife* may have difficulty liking an ex-wife? Historically, the conclusion has been that this enmity is some kind of woman cat-fight, spurred by jealousy. The assumption was that the *next-wife's* dislike must have been provoked solely by territorial issues, and not because the ex-wife had actually ever done physical, emotional, or financial harm to the *next-wife.*

It's time to come out of the closet about such misperceptions! Granted, many ex-wives are decent human beings, good mothers, and shining examples of womanhood at its finest. However, others are the accumulative total of the scenarios described, plus some. You probably have unique stories about your own ex-wife, that even exceed the limits of what's been covered in this guide!

The domineering, critical stepmother has been the prominent image of the *next-wife* for decades. But it's time the ex-wife becomes accountable for the damage her resentment and need to control has done to her children, to her ex-husband, to the *next-wife,* and to anyone else who happened to get in her way.

Many *next-wives* want to find it within their hearts to like their ex-wife, if for no other reason than their shared gender. And simply the fact that the *next-wife* will regularly spend time with the stepchild, should encourage the former wife to develop an amicable relationship with this new woman. But alas, that's usually not the case.

A *next-wife* cannot control an ex-wife, any more than the opposite is true. You don't have to like her or her actions, and you certainly don't have to be her friend. She truly may not possess the depth of character that you require from your close associates. Just make sure that your feelings do not overtake your good sense and moral conviction. Don't succumb to her provocations, and resist retaliating in like manner.

Step onto the moral high ground and refuse to strike back. Never deride her to her children, and spare your new husband the onslaught of your verbal attack against her. And when you see her, smile sweetly and inquire how she is. Even though you already know.

Chapter Nine:

RATS!
Remarriage Ain't
The Same

Survival Ex-ism #9

EXcel

It may not be your dream game
Or one that gets reviews,
But this game you'll *excel* in;
If only you choose.

 100

Your belief in happily-ever-after disintegrated faster than the ink could dry on your divorce decree. After the heartache and disappointment of your failed marriage, you realized there was no such creature as your soul mate. Too late, you discovered that Prince Charming could only be found on storybook pages, and in the expectant hearts of naïve young women. Your naiveté followed your ex-husband right out the door. Older but wiser, you'd sworn you'd never fall for the fallacy of everlasting love again.

But then you met *him*. Suddenly, you felt as if you were a sixteen-year-old girl experiencing her first crush. Could it really be that *this* man was your destiny? Hope welled up inside you, and burst forth in an optimism that'd been buried since the dissolution of your former marriage. Had you simply made an error in judgment before? Could the fairy tale be viable, after all? In spite of your hard-earned wisdom, you threw caution to the wind and plunged headlong into love again.

And he was perfect for you! You'd even shared similar physical, emotional, and possibly financial, destruction in the wake of your individual divorces. You understood one another's needs, and were all too eager to meet each and every one of them. You basked in being loved again, and reciprocated by showering him with accolades and affection. Life was good.

So you decided to make it even better, and waded into the precarious waters of wedded bliss—again. Only this time, you were confident that you'd both learned what it'd take to promote a healthy, loving remarriage, that would indeed, survive a lifetime.

You've probably operated under the assumption that a remarriage is the same as a marriage, just a "do-over" with another person. Since the prefix "re" means *again*, technically, that definition would be true. But realistically, it couldn't be further from it. There is no repeating an original marriage, except possibly if you remarry your original partner. Just as you get only one chance at making a good first impression, you get only *one* first marriage.

So let's consider for a moment what's common between these two entities. First, a man and woman commit before God and witnesses, their undying love to the spouse. They promise fidelity. Nurturance. Companionship.

Now, assuming there's living parents and siblings, they'll each acquire in-laws, as well as the accompanying extended family members.

But here is where the similarities abruptly end. In a first marriage, if both partners desire children, they'll enjoy their newlywed status while anticipating the future lives their love will create. And when that time comes, they'll share the joy together of how Suzy's precocious flair for fashion is just like her mommy, and how little Johnny's passion for gourmet cooking fell straight off his old dad's block.

In a remarriage, chances are the past love of your new husband and his ex-wife, lives on in the form of their child or children. And possibly, you'd also created a little wonder of your own with your former husband. So if you and your new husband desire to create a love child together, it'll be as an addition to the ready-made family your union has already forged. No honeymoon anticipatory period. Just a new husband and a new wife, now stepparents as well as original parents, creating the miracle of life that will prove their love exists. But sadly, this innocent baby may also become the object of scorn and jealousy from its half-siblings, further complicating your fragile blended family unity.

Even if you decide that your family is complete with just the children you each brought to the union, numerous differences still plague the institution of remarriage. Many of those anomalies have already been exposed in previous chapters. There's the difficulty of children you're responsible for, yet don't have the authority to truly "parent." Or your new husband's extended family won't accept that they're now legally related to you. Meanwhile, you're literally tripping in his ex-wife's footsteps. You struggle to catch the cadence of your new husband's ex-*life*, which you've slowly come to recognize is also your *current* life. You constantly fight the demons of his past acquaintances and memories. And you're haunted by the echo of mistaken names he's whispered in the night.

However, one major difference between marriage and remarriage that hasn't been mentioned earlier, is in the area of finances. Because remarriage often happens after one or both of the partners have experienced some level of success in their chosen career or profession, often that partner brings a sizeable financial contribution to the new union. And even though you may very likely be the one who is more financially stable, for the purpose of this scenario, we will assume that it's *him* that holds that status.

And that's a good thing, right? Every woman wants a man who is able to carry his own weight and wallet. Ah, but the golden goose may not be nesting just yet! Your new husband's bank account had been ravaged by his ex, and he still feels violated. He'd limped away from his divorce settlement like a dog that was thrown a gnawed-on bone. The meat was gone, but the scent of what once was, remained to taunt him.

By the time you met him, he had a good start on rebuilding his financial dreams. His wounds were healing. However, he would forever be leery of trusting a woman near his money again.

But your new love had exemplified generosity and selflessness from the start. It was one of the characteristics you loved most about him. He wasn't just generous with *you*, he genuinely cared when others were in need, and gave often and freely to help whenever he could. He sponsored several hungry children in impoverished countries, and volunteered to help build houses in his own community, which would become someone's first opportunity at owning the American Dream.

But then, just as you were beginning to talk of forever together, seemingly out of the blue, he verbalized the ugly "P" word. That's right. Just when you'd thought your dream man was in fact, flesh and blood and not some fantasy, he vaporized with just one utterance—*prenup*.

So how does a future *next-wife* survive this setback? First, wipe off the dazed look on your face. Next, calm your pounding heart, and reign in your racing emotions. Take a deep breath, and turn down the heat on your anger that's threatening to boil over. After all, this isn't really about you. It's about him, and his protectiveness, his ego, or simply his unwillingness to commit all of himself to his soon-to-be bride.

And before you go storming off in a huff, you should first consider the precarious sand a remarriage is built upon. Regardless of how in-love you feel now, the stark fact can't be ignored that your union may fail. And statistically, that failure would happen before your fifth anniversary. He has a legitimate right to be concerned that if that fate should befall your remarriage, he could lose half of the half he managed to keep last time.

But simply acknowledging his prudence in being cautious, doesn't excuse what I consider to be his attempt at *collaging* the new union. I've coined the word *collaging*, to describe what happens when the appealing pieces of the remarriage are kept (sex, companionship, free nursing services when sick), while the undesirable section (primarily sharing worldly wealth), is cut out and discarded. In this way, the collage creates the illusion of a total commitment to onlookers, though it's two-dimensional and lacks depth. Meanwhile, he gets all the benefits of having you as his *next-wife*, with none of the risks he encountered with his ex-wife.

It's true that when a couple remarries, they immediately become equal partners in the eyes of the law, and one flesh according to scripture. However, actual meshing doesn't happen overnight, but is worked out through time. Perhaps there is justification for a prenup to be in force for a certain number of years. Or maybe not.

I still believe that it signifies that one of the partners isn't willing to totally commit to the remarriage. The order of protection called *prenup* is a one-way street, designed exclusively for the preservation of just one spouse. It probably stipulates that in the event of divorce, the assets are to be divided a certain way—he gets everything he brought to the remarriage.

But what if you work and increase the standard of living for both of you? How do you divide what each of you contributes to the union? And if you read the fine print, there's probably no protection for you if *he*'s the one who strays, or decides he didn't mean forever, after all. You would've been acting in good faith toward the coupling, while he could just walk away, unblemished.

To me, a prenuptial agreement is no agreement at all. It's a guerilla tactic that twists the arm of the *next-wife*, into seeing things her future husband's way. It's a cleverly disguised attempt to change the very essence of what remarriage—any marriage—is about, and that's being totally committed to your partner. You can't be just a little bit married, any more than a woman can be just a little bit pregnant. You're either married, or you're not. Anything less than a full commitment is nothing more than a childish attempt at playing house. If that's his desire (or yours), perhaps remarriage isn't for you, after all.

Ultimately, only you can decide whether or not to sign a prenup. But if you have any reservations about doing so, yet do it anyway in the name of love—beware!

Yet you scoff at the warning. A prenup is

activated only in the case of divorce, and since your perfect relationship will never end up there, it's really a moot point, right?

Wrong! In the back of your mind, you'll always be aware that he didn't love you enough to share equally with you. Or he didn't respect your character enough to trust, that even if your union fell prey to the statistics, you would never resort to the lows that his ex-wife had stooped to in their divorce.

This truth can fester between the two of you like a malignant tumor. In this case, the truth will not set you free. Its poison grows with each passing day, and won't retreat until it has destroyed the love you once shared.

Where There's a Will, There's a Way...His!

There's nothing romantic about preparing your will, yet most parents endure this unpleasant task in order to protect their children in the event of their death. It's the mature, responsible, and right thing to do. However, preparing a will in a remarriage can remind you—none too gently—that the entity called remarriage, will never quite measure up to its predecessor.

Miranda and Bob are a case in point. Bob is fifteen years older than Miranda, and they each have a son from previous relationships, Sean and Hank.

Sean was ten-years-old when his mother

married Bob, and since Miranda had custody, he lived with his mom and stepdad full-time. Sean's natural father rarely picked him up for visits, so Bob quickly became a second father to him.

Bob's own son, Hank, was seventeen at the time of the remarriage, and visits with his dad had already become sporadic. The father/son relationship was still intact, but Bob had begun experiencing what most parents of teenagers face eventually. Weekends with Dad had been traded for dates with his girlfriend, or for cruising around in his pickup truck.

So from the very beginning, Miranda and Bob's blended family included primarily Sean. And Miranda had often marveled at her good fortune. Bob had been a wonderful husband to her and a father-figure for her son, and the years slipped happily by.

But as good fortunes often do, Miranda's crashed when she and her husband decided to update their wills. In this case, Bob's premarital nest egg had far surpassed Miranda's meager savings account, and even after ten years together, Bob still considered this money to be *his alone*. Therefore, only two people could be considered as his legitimate heirs—Miranda and Hank.

Miranda's heart sank. Bob hadn't included provisions for Sean. By now her son was twenty, but Hank was twenty-seven, so she didn't think their ages could've played a part in Bob's decision.

She reminded her husband that she was his

legal wife—complete with joint bank accounts. His former money had become theirs. Yet she'd never taken advantage of that fact, and had worked hard in her career in the banking industry. They'd shared household expenses, and dreamed together of how their money would provide a comfortable retirement for both of them.

Before Miranda met her husband, she'd struggled as a single mother to raise her child and make ends meet. Meanwhile, Bob had made wise investments in the stock market, roping in the bulls of the early dot-com craze. He'd reaped a bundle, then walked out of the Wall Street arena like a triumphant matador.

She knew Bob had made "his" money legally and ethically, but Miranda resented his attitude about it. He hadn't earned it by the sweat of his brow, even though it'd resulted from some of his savvy decisions. But as far as she was concerned, he'd been *blessed* with it. It wasn't exactly like he'd won it, but it was close. And because of that, her skin crawled as she watched him guard it like a lion protecting his kill.

Miranda had naturally assumed that if she and Bob died in a joint tragedy, both sons would inherit half of the estate. But that's not the way Bob saw it. Once again, he stood firm on the justification that it'd been *his* money before he'd met Miranda. And he reasoned that since Sean's father had not consistently paid child support, Bob had taken up the slack and provided financially for the child, as if he were his own. Therefore, he believed he'd more than fulfilled his obligations as Sean's stepfather.

Miranda couldn't argue that point. She agreed that her husband had been an ideal stepdad to her son. That's exactly why Bob's plans for "his" estate had caught her off guard.

Then her husband admitted that although if he passed away first, he wanted Hank to have half of all he owned, he didn't believe Miranda's premature death should warrant the same inheritance for her son. Why should her child inherit half of everything Bob had worked so hard for? Well, even if he hadn't actually worked for it in the usual sense, it was still his. And he planned on using it to carry him through retirement. He couldn't afford for Sean to inherit a penny of it.

However, Bob reasoned that in the event of *his* premature death, half of the estate should be sufficient for his widow. Miranda's relative youth would enable her to continue to work to supplement her retirement income. Whereas, if she died before he did, Bob wouldn't have the luxury of that option at his age.

Obviously, Bob and Miranda had some serious problems to iron out, and they weren't financial ones, either. It wasn't actually the money that was at issue here. Rather, it was Bob's refusal to accept that unless they had legally agreed earlier that it was *not* joint property (there's that prenup issue popping up again!), the money was indeed, also his wife's. Many states have a common property provision guaranteeing joint ownership of assets between spouses.

Bob wasn't a demon just because he'd wanted to leave his only child a sizeable inheritance. But neither was Miranda out of line in believing that all of their assets were jointly shared, and should be considered likewise in their estate planning.

Miranda couldn't argue that her financial contribution to their union was no match for Bob's assets. But that didn't mean she hadn't brought many valuable attributes to the remarriage. Bob's acquaintances had remarked how he'd seemed to come alive after he'd met her. In his *next-wife's* presence, Bob had discovered irrepressible laughter, sparked by simply sharing a joke that was understood by only the two of them. And he'd experienced true contentment for the first time, birthed from the unconditional love his life's partner freely lavished upon him.

Some things cannot be measured by the almighty dollar. Fortunately, Bob and Miranda sought counseling (for their relationship, not their finances) and they were finally able to arrive at a mutually agreeable inheritance for both of their children.

It should be obvious to you by now that

believing remarriage is the same as a first marriage, is like thinking the reflection in the glass is truly you. Go ahead. Touch it. You'll see that it's just a well-disguised imposter. Rushing forward without first recognizing this illusion, has resulted in more than one banged-up head...and countless broken hearts.

Although marriage and remarriage are two distinct entities, it's likely that many of the same challenges that existed in your first one, will also surface in this new union. There are the usual issues of intimacy versus withdrawal, fights over how to spend or save money, disagreements over disciplining the children, and personality conflicts in general. Heap on the additional complications of dealing with past lives that can't be ignored, and the struggle in a remarriage can be all uphill.

It would seem that a logical person would rather be thrown into a snake pit, than into a remarriage! And yet, statistics say that ninety-five percent of all divorced persons eventually remarry. Love is a powerful emotion, and it brings with it a seemingly invincible spirit. It's convincing in its insistence that you and your new beloved can surely beat the odds.

And to put a positive spin on another statistic, twenty-four percent of second marriages do survive. However, the odds drop to a thirteen percent success rate if you're in your third try, and plummets to a dismal seven percent chance that a fourth attempt will endure past five years. *Sigh*

That may not sound like much, but at least it's something. And you can increase your odds by being aware of the pitfalls experienced by others. You can seek help early and often, for guidance on issues that have the potential to split your new union wide open, usually along the biological lines of your children.

The resources that deal with common remarriage issues listed at the back of this book, include websites and an on-line chat group. There may be a blended family ministry or support group in your community that you could join, as well. If no such group exists, consider creating one yourself. Contact area churches, nonprofit organizations, or family counseling centers, to see if they could help.

And most of all, you can avoid bitter disappointment by not expecting remarriage to be something it isn't, namely just a second chance at a first marriage. See it for what it is—a coupling with someone you love, but who brought as much, if not more, baggage to your union than you did. Your remarriage must bear past burdens, as well as the new ones it inadvertently created. At times it may seem as if you'll suffocate from the weight of it. Sadly, the burden does break the backs of many hopeful remarriages.

So why even try? That's like asking why bother to breathe. The answer is simple, really. We are created for love. And for companionship. Genesis

2:18 states, *"The Lord God said, 'It is not good for the man to be alone. I will make a helper suitable for him.'"* (NIV) (This author believes the Biblical reference to man, also includes *wo*-man.)

Life is meant to be shared. And for many, the most rewarding arena in which to experience this sharing, is within the intimate bonds of matrimony. So when you struck out the first time, you decided that it wasn't the end of the game. You could still play, you could even win, you'd just have to keep swinging.

But as you stepped up to that matrimonial plate the second time around, you had the sensation of being in a dream. The players were vaguely recognizable, and yet you couldn't recall their names. You walked out onto the familiar field, but as you dug in your heels to position yourself at bat, you suddenly became aware of the dirt around your feet. You felt it mound around your ankles, and then it rose up to your shins. RATS! You were sinking! Your dream was turning into a nightmare!

Just then the ball was pitched and you swung with all the strength you could muster. The *splat!* of your bat connected solidly. It was music to your ears, and serenaded you toward first base.

You ran freely—thrilled to be back in the game—and you realized something. Remarriage may not be the same as an original marriage, but you've begun to like the game you're playing. And as you rounded these bases, you were aware that you'd never felt such exhilaration! Your adrenaline pumped as you spied home base.

Home. Your home with your new husband. The one created by this mysterious phenomenon called remarriage.

Chapter Ten:

First At Last!

Survival Ex-ism #10

Exult

Things aren't always easy
Will you figure it out?
Exult in being the *next-wife*
Love is what it's about.

Finally, you've accepted your lot in life. You're the *next-wife*. And in so becoming, you've developed the endurance of an Olympic athlete, the finesse of a ballerina, and the patience of Job (the Biblical icon for suffering).

You've mixed jealousy with security, anger with pride, sadness and joy, relief and turmoil—and that's just within one day! The medical and psychiatric fields are perplexed that you've experienced all of these emotions and more, simultaneously and in rapid succession. Their prognosis is that you epitomize an as-of-yet undiagnosed malady, or perhaps some bizarre form of Bipolar Disorder, that has metamorphosed into *quadruple*-polar, and beyond. But you just smile knowingly, anxious for that day when everyone will recognize the symptoms of being the *next-wife*.

So is your condition fatal? Well, it certainly killed off any childhood fantasies about what marriage—remarriage, in your case—would entail. But nature is a perpetual creator also, birthing new dreams from the ashes of old ones. Funny, but the challenges you've overcome and the obstacles still remaining, aren't as daunting as they once seemed. You've learned how to navigate the treacherous terrain of this brave, new world you've embarked upon. And even though any mistaken step could spell disaster, you've grown accustomed to the thrill of being the *next-wife*.

What other woman—through dogged persistence and determination—could finally win the trust and affection of a wary stepchild? And who else could grin graciously as she hands her husband the phone, with yet another unnecessary call from his ex-wife, that was meant to intrude upon her time and home?

Only the *next-wife*. You're a unique breed, and you are to be celebrated. Perhaps you breathed a sigh of relief as you identified with these scenarios from other *next-wives*. You aren't alone, after all. The feelings you've struggled with are natural, and are an integral part of the *next-wife* species.

Eventually, the unrealistic expectations you'd held dear when you remarried, are replaced by an abiding security in the love you and your new husband have maintained—in spite of excruciatingly difficult obstacles. And it's that love and commitment to each other that is truly the key to thriving in your remarriage.

All the children will eventually grow up and leave the nest, just as in original marriages. Then it will be only you and your husband. And if you weren't successful in correlating simultaneous visitation schedules for both sets of kids, it may be the first time in your union that you've had the house all to yourself!

So don't make the mistake of neglecting the reason you became a *next-wife* in the first place— your husband, and your relationship together. You may have heard the expression that the riper the fruit, the sweeter the juice? Well, your relationship will have had time to ripen over the years if you've remembered to tend to it. And if you've taken to heart some of the experiences in this book, hopefully you can start to enjoy the hard-earned and well-deserved fruits of being the *next-wife.*

The apostle Paul writes in 1 Corinthians 9:24, *"Do you not know that in a race all the runners run, but only one gets the prize? Run in such a way as to get the prize."* (NIV)

Sounds simple enough, doesn't it? But is being *first* the coveted prize Paul describes? Jesus told a parable in Matthew 20:16 and concluded with these words, *"So the last will be first, and the first will be last."* (NIV)

In other words, you may not have been the first wife, and you've officially been known throughout these pages as the *next-wife.* But you can strive for something even greater still, and that is to be his *last* wife! For she who finishes last— wins!

Additional Resources

Plans fail for lack of counsel,
but with many advisers they succeed.

Proverbs 15:22 (NIV)

Additional Resources

Books:
God Breathes on Blended Families,
Moe and Paige Becnel
Published by Healing Place Productions, Inc.
www.blendingAfamily.com

The Smart Step-Family, Ron L. Deal
Published by Bethany House Publishers
www.successfulstepfamilies.com

Stepcoupling, Susan Wisdom, LPC, and
Jennifer Green
Published by Three Rivers Press

Emotional Blackmail, Susan Forward, Ph.D.
Published by Quill
(An Imprint of Harper-Collins Publishers)

Websites:
Second Wives Club
www.secondwivesclub.com

Stepfamily Association of America
www.stepfam.org

Stepfamily Foundation
www.stepfamily.org

Paula J. Egner
Speaks Out!

Topics Include:

DIVORCE:
Disaster or Deliverance?

RATS!
Remarriage Ain't The Same

DEPRESSION:
Death in Disguise?

BIPOLAR:
From Pits to Paradise

Paula's unique style of blending harsh reality with the healing salve of humor, is like inhaling a gulp of pure oxygen with dawn's first light. At once fresh and exhilarating, she delivers truth with empathetic candor. Her insight reflects one who's not only been there, but *IS* there! She strives to enlighten, to encourage, and to educate women everywhere. To book Paula for your group or association, or to request more information, including rates, log onto our website:

www.AptlySpoken.net
(Click on Topics of Interest)